THE BLACK OCEAN

CRAB ORCHARD SERIES IN POETRY
OPEN COMPETITION AWARD

THE BLACK OCEAN

BRIAN BARKER

CRAB ORCHARD REVIEW &
SOUTHERN ILLINOIS UNIVERSITY PRESS
CARBONDALE AND EDWARDSVILLE

14 13 12 11   4 3 2 1

The Crab Orchard Series in Poetry is a joint publishing venture
of Southern Illinois University Press and *Crab Orchard Review*.
This series has been made possible by the generous support of
the Office of the President of Southern Illinois University and
the Office of the Vice Chancellor for Academic Affairs and Pro-
vost at Southern Illinois University Carbondale.

Crab Orchard Series in Poetry Editor: Jon Tribble
Open Competition Award Judge for 2010: Michael Waters

Library of Congress Cataloging-in-Publication Data
Barker, Brian, [date]
The black ocean / Brian Barker.
    p. cm. — (Crab Orchard series in poetry)
ISBN-13: 978-0-8093-3028-7 (pbk. : alk. paper)
ISBN-10: 0-8093-3028-8 (pbk. : alk. paper)
ISBN-13: 978-0-8093-8631-4 (ebook)
ISBN-10: 0-8093-8631-3 (ebook)
I. Title. II . Series.
PS3602.A77547B53 2011
811'.6—dc22
2010040795

Printed on recycled paper. ♻
The paper used in this publication meets the minimum require-
ments of American National Standard for Information Sciences—
Permanence of Paper for Printed Library Materials, ANSI Z39.48-
1992. ∞

For Nicky—
who sings to me in the dark

CONTENTS

Acknowledgments   ix

Dragging Canoe Vanishes from the Bear Pit into
    the Endless Clucking of the Gods   1

*

Visions for the Last Night on Earth   16

Poe Climbs Down from the Long Tapestry of Death to Command
    an Army of Street Urchins Huddled in the Dusk   17

Lullaby for the Last Night on Earth   23

The Last Songbird   24

*

Gorbachev's Ubi Sunt from the Future That Soon Will Pass   28

Silent Montage with Late Reagan in Black and White   34

Love Poem for the Last Night on Earth   37

In the City of Fallen Rebels   38

*

Lost on the Lost Shores of New Orleans, They Dreamed Abraham
    Lincoln Was the Magician of the Great Divide   42

Field Recording, Notes from the Machine   47

Visions for the Last Night on Earth   49

Field Recording, Billie Holiday from the Far Edge of Heaven   50

Nightmare for the Last Night on Earth   51

*

A Brief Oral Account of Torture Pulled Down Out of the Wind   54

Notes   65

ACKNOWLEDGMENTS

Thanks to the editors of the following journals, where many of the poems in this book first appeared, sometimes in different versions or under different titles:

Anti-: "Love Poem for the Last Night on Earth"
Fugue: "Poe Climbs Down from the Long Tapestry of Death to
    Command an Army of Street Urchins Huddled in the Dusk"
Jabberwock Review: "Field Recording, Billie Holiday
    from the Far Edge of Heaven"
Kenyon Review Online: "Silent Montage with Late Reagan in Black and White"
Memorious: "In the City of Fallen Rebels," "Field Recording,
    Notes from the Machine," and "The Last Songbird"
Pleiades: "Lullaby for the Last Night on Earth," "Gorbachev's Ubi Sunt from
    the Future That Soon Will Pass," "Nightmare for the Last Night on Earth,"
    and "A Brief Oral Account of Torture Pulled Down Out of the Wind"
Sou'wester: "Lost on the Lost Shores of New Orleans, They Dreamed
    Abraham Lincoln Was the Magician of the Great Divide"
storySouth: "Dragging Canoe Vanishes from the Bear
    Pit into the Endless Clucking of the Gods"
Triquarterly: "Visions for the Last Night on Earth"
    ("Then I saw the floodwaters recede . . .")
Waccamaw: "Visions for the Last Night on Earth"
    ("That spring the wind smelled . . .")

"Dragging Canoe Vanishes from the Bear Pit into the Endless Clucking of the Gods," "Nightmare for the Last Night on Earth," and "A Brief Oral Account of Torture Pulled Down Out of the Wind" won the 2009 Campbell Corner Poetry Prize. Thanks to the judges for honoring my work.

Thanks to Jon Tribble for reading this manuscript with such care, and to Michael Waters for believing in these poems. Thanks too to everyone at Southern Illinois University Press for their good work in preparing this book for publication.

Thanks to all of those who have encouraged me during the writing of this book through deed, word, and spirit, especially Murray Farish, Sean Hill, Rodney Jones, Judy Jordan, Andy McFadyen-Ketchum, Wayne Miller, Keith Montesano, Catherine Pierce, Kevin Prufer, and Jake Adam York.

And, as always, I owe a deep debt of gratitude to my wife, Nicky Beer, who was the first to read these poems and offer advice, and who first said that being married to another poet was like cheating.

THE BLACK OCEAN

Dragging Canoe Vanishes from the Bear Pit into
the Endless Clucking of the Gods

Before we are forgotten, we will be turned into kitsch. Kitsch is the stopover
between being and oblivion.

                                                    —Milan Kundera

Those six bears in the pit behind the moccasin shop
pad all summer on a narrow path of shade,
panting, swaying,
                  stopping to stand tall on two legs and bellow

when the god-faces bob in the heat beyond the iron rail,

featureless puckers of milky light
that cluck and whistle and holler, flaunting
candy apples, funnel cakes,
saltwater taffy in twisted wax wrappers—

anything that might mingle hunger and curiosity—

though the bears know neither,
know only the pacing that links their days
in a tether of sliding fat,

and the stillness of the pit at night
when the gods step back into darkness,
when the shellacked stones swallow the sun

and they collapse beneath their own weight at last . . .

Already the wheezing warrior has swept up
the day's garbage
                  and vanished up the boulevard

toward the neon rigging, the kiss of cold air
behind the glass at Harrah's.
Already the stars have wheeled into place
over the teenagers huddled behind the strip mall,
smoking beneath the peeling billboard

where de Soto sits his horse above the town,
squinting through a spyglass,
the mountains in the background
brushed with the gauzy-blue mist of dusk.

                              *

Discover the Wonders of Cherokee, the billboard read,

and another hand-painted sign, roadside:
Have your photo taken with Dragging Canoe—
Fierce Warrior, Bear Tamer.

We posed in front of a yellow sheetmetal teepee.
I was six. I grinned sheepishly beneath an oversized baseball cap,
his left hand on my shoulder, the right
pressing a hatchet flat against his chest.

A faded headdress swung down his back,
and he squinted,
staring past the camera,
past the souvenir stands, the miniature
golf courses and bingo parlors,
past the pit to our left where the gods clucked

and the bears bellowed
beneath sporadic showers of sugar and grease.

In that moment, when the flash flared,
when the camera cradled us in its plastic eye
                              before blinking us back—

[my striped tube socks drawn to my knees; his belly bulging, a brown
moon, and a pack of Marlboros snug in the elastic band of the shorts he
wore beneath deerskin pants]

in that moment, even then,
the bears' teeth were rotting, their brittle claws
were splintering on the hot cement;
their muzzles were grizzling, the whites of their eyes
pooled with bilirubin; blood was seeping
from their gums, their lungs funneled phlegm;
globules of blubber multiplied, orbiting their livers,
sheathing their hearts, buttery nuggets
sucking the sheen out of their glossy coats.

*

I held the Polaroid—

I held a stuffed bear—

I held a yellow mug full of Mamaw Mulligan's World Famous Fudge—

I ate the fudge and then the mug held seven plastic arrowheads and a penny—

I held the penny—
        [I placed it, carefully, on the silver tongue and fed it to the machine. The
        gears turned on their greased axles. Each tooth met its mate.]

I held my mother's hand—
        [The machine whirred. It was magic, or progress, and my father kept saying,
        Would you look at that? Would you just look at that?]

I held the penny, transformed, polished and oblong, stamped with a family of
        bears—

I held cotton candy and rock candy—
        [My fingers were sugar. I wanted to touch the bears' pink lips.]

I held a leather belt, my name stitched in miniature turquoise beads—
    [Someone could spell me. I existed.]

I held the village floating in a glass globe—
    [It was quiet. It was empty and filling with snow.]

I held the Polaroid—
    [Until the teepee melted and the boy's face sloshed like milk from beneath
    his cap.]

*

Being's a vagabond—
               It shows itself in its absence—

It steps out into the snow
billowing over the Long Island of the Holston,

the snow tracing its thousand shapes,
spiraling, drifting into the ancient
branches of the pines that separate them
and sweep them clean.

It coughs and curls up next to the river clogged with ice.
It slips into gaudy costumes to stay warm
and walks the streets, rinsed in benzene, muttering abstractions . . .

To become something you can't touch,
a curiosity, something

theatrical, not quite bear, not quite man,
parading in circles around the abandoned cul-de-sac
of history, as the ice cries out beneath your steps
like fingerbones,

        as the branches snicker together
and the bayonet blades point the way deeper
into what's already sunk in winter:

toy animals and toy tomahawks
asleep, floating in the dark that blots

the shop windows, the snow like famine
touching the casino's stained awning,

touching the eyelashes of those who lost,

touching the chainlink mouths and the dim
half-forgotten meals spilling from a dumpster . . .

To be nobody. To be a whole clan or nation.
To be, in the end, both at once.

*

If you heard crying on the wind,
it wasn't me but the warrior in the men's room stall,

his moccasins framed
in the sour rectangle of light
beneath the door.

How far did I follow him with my penny
in my fist, watching him wind through the crowd,
his shoulders heaving?

How far did I follow him?
Past the artificial waterfalls and ramshackle motels
blistering with bright paint?

Past the casino like a ship of glass
marooned in the mountains?

He shed his feathers, his deerskin pants.
He chucked his hatchet into the kudzu.

He walked the shoulder of the road
like a tightrope, into the long-leaf pines,
where the pearly scent of wild onions
floats above the river
                              and clings to the locust-light,
to a basket of black hair swimming with silt.

                              *

(The Chiefs Remember)

They shuffled words—

They shuffled cups, bottomless cups—
        [Rum roiled like a gluttonous river.]

They shuffled time—
        [Day swung from their gold chains. Night was swaddled in their wool
        pockets.]

They shuffled us—
        [We were marked cards smuggled up their sleeves.]

They shuffled their faces—
        [One touched his moustache and laughed. Darkness fluttered out of his
        pocket like a moth. It flit on the tip of a candle flame.]

They shuffled the treaty of a treaty of a treaty—
        [Birds darted into their secret rooms. Trees shuddered and turned white.]

They shuffled Xs—
        [We were Xs. We were blown musketsmoke.]

They shuffled him—

[But he was young. He rose and stomped the ground. His anger was a furious wind dismantling the dark.]

They shuffled smiles—

[They put on their hats and strolled off into the forest, into *their* forest. They forgot it all and emptied into streets, strolled past leather shops and candy shops, past the casino.]

They shuffled his breath—

[He was chain-smoking at the slots, a cup of quarters cradled between his knees. Each time he pulled the lever he held his breath, waiting for what hung in the air behind it to come clattering down.]

They shuffled his flesh—

[There was so much of him now, it spilled over the waistband of his sweatpants. How did we know him? He wore a softball jersey with his name silk-screened on the back.]

They shuffled their feet over sidewalks—

[There were too many to count. They clucked. Their faces were featureless. A young one said, *Where are all the Indians?* The father said, *Look*, and pointed. Two bears were standing on their heads in a dumpster.]

They shuffled the wind—

[There was no wind, only silence buried in the putty his body had become. Only feathers of sweat fanning from beneath his arms.]

They shuffled us—

[We were so far away. We were falling through his breath.]

They shuffled beauty—

[He uncrumpled a twenty and Andrew Jackson glared back. Smug and regal, lantern-jawed, a bit bemused. His hair swept back off his forehead. Like waves of fire. Like a fashion model's.]

*

Bear touched back to salt—

        Bear on the wind—

Bear beneath the river
            in the shoal-swirl and turtle-oar—

Coughing Bear
        suffocating at the end of summer,

when the trees fold their green tents
and the hides are stretched, hung up dripping—

Bear of Polymer—
           Bear of the Gone Gall-Bladder and the Halo of Flies—

    Bear of Sugar, eating its own lips—

Bear of Gunmetal and Glue—

Bear of Air—
        Bear of the Ten Tongues bellowing in the air,

tangled in a rope ladder, swaying

            in the middle of the pit,

a palsied pendulum, a hiccup in the sky,
the cement twenty feet below, a jar of peanut butter
ten feet above, tied to the clapper of a bell—

    Come down to me
    Bear of Memory, Bear of Hurt,
    carry me crying into the cattails
    where they've slept, untouched,
    for thousands of nights.

Come down to me,
with your warm hug and your fur
I could bury my face in, a pelt of sleep,
an old suitcase of smells—

something I could curl into,
                    and pull the lid down, my cheeks burning . . .

                              *

So long Old Hickory, you sharp-knifed son-of-a-bitch,

Dragging Canoe thinks, descending deeper

      into the ravine behind his breath, through a neon mist,

through tear gas and acid rain

      gnawing at the edges of the mountain ridges as he poses

with one child, then another,

      cataleptic, the visions unspooling beyond it all

spun by the carousel of buzzards

      above the dry pines, above the *mock-mock-mock* of a bayonet

dragged across the stockade slats,

      where a woman kneels to pick corn kernels from the dirt,

her baby slung snug against her, its cries

      splitting her breasts against the rhythm of the blade

she'd like to drive through the soldier's chest,

      although he means nothing by it, is just a kid, is just in love

with himself and bored of standing

guard, of watching the wide swaths of smoke rise

over the mountains, carrying the houses and barns

and fields on fire, carrying the offices of the *Phoenix* burning down—

So long ghost-hand, he thinks, as it flutters, as it fans behind his eyes, the blankets

stacked like cards, the sick Queen in the hole, small pox,

whooping cough, dysentery, tongues

swollen, lips pocked with ulcers. Just last week, a grandmother

with a little tatter of Kleenex in her fist

touched his elbow, called him *Dear*, asked if he spoke

English, and he imagined, for a moment,

how easily her blue hair, her waxy skin would peel

back from her skull, even with his rubber hatchet,

even not knowing the technique, how to hold

the bloody thing up to the sun or what scream

might make the gods human again, their knees gone wobbly,

their hearts jostling in their stomachs as they run—

But it's too late, he knows. History's the gash the bootheel left,

the gash language leaked out of, so that now,

when the teenagers beneath the billboard pass the pipe

[the chemical ember winking in the glass

bowl like a cooling star], they pass it in silence, always to the right

in order not to lose their place, pass it

all through spring and into summer, season of exodus,

the soldiers rising in the glacial light of dawn,

yawning, scratching their chests, pissing on the campfires

to douse the dying coals—

So long wind, so long crows, he thinks, as trees buckle,

as roads muscle up through

dynamite grooves, the Palace of Burgers and the Palace of Cards

strung on a dull constellation of rivets,

trailers shimmed with cinderblocks above a current of shale,

whole families of bears trampling out

of rhododendrons to stand roadside, backing the traffic up,

swaying back and forth a bit, their forepaws raised

for balance, their pink tongues licking their lips.

[The gods cluck and throw in six-packs of beer,

melted motherboards, bloated road kill; they throw in milky condoms

and rusted out carburetors;

they throw in shells of televisions, bicycle handlebars, spent

shotgun cartridges, cigarette butts and tattoo needles.]

So long Dragging Canoe, he thinks, as he squints, or winces,

each thing plummeting inside him

when he places his hand on the shoulder of the boy and steps

out of himself into his own gaze,

into an abandoned camp to touch a muddy sandal and a newspaper

crumpled on a pallet, to touch a clump of gray hair

tangled in a brush, just before the flash flares and the bodies

are slipped into the river like empty boats.

*

I held the warrior
                 until the novelty wore off,

the Polaroid stuffed in my back pocket
where the colors crumbled and the details
sweated out in a wet chemical paste. ·

Now the boy is a streak of carmine,
the teepee a sulfur smear
along one edge, the warrior floating
in the middle of the frame, a blue
blur of static I lean over tonight and study.

I want to stare at this mist until he's whole again.
I want to set him in motion for once,

there, on the other side, where a transistor radio
bleats across the floodlit pit.
He's slipped out of his costume
and out of his name,
                 humming through his cigarette,
swaying, sidestepping
as he sweeps
so his sweeping becomes a kind of dance.

Flakes of dung and tufts of fur tread the air
as he stomps, as he shuffles around the bears
asleep on the cement, their tongues
hanging half out, their bodies twitching
in dream and after-dream.

He throws his back into it

      and lifts his left leg high and sets it down—
      and lifts his right leg high and sets it down—

Blood ringing like bells through his swollen ankles,
the bears jerking in time with his steps . . .

Beyond the rock and iron rail, the town is burning down.
He feels it coming apart, spreading in hot eddies

beneath his skin: the casino going up
in a breath of sparks and shattered glass,

the billboard wavering
on its tinder stilts, the scaffolding collapsing,
de Soto breaking away on umbrellas of ash.

But here, now,
                    the air is clear and empty

and holds them, man and bears, as the pit sinks
to blackness beneath their shapes I trace.

If I lean over the edge
                    I can almost touch them.

        They are thin
                    and light as snow now . . .

        Now they are nothing.

*

Visions for the Last Night on Earth

Then I saw the floodwaters recede, leaving a milky scum
scalloped on silos and billboards, and the eaves of farmhouses
were festooned with a mossy brown riverweed
that hung in the August heat like bankers' limp fingers,
and the drowned corn, sick from sewage and tidesuck,
reappeared like a washed-out green ocean of wilting speartips
that bloated fish rode into the moonlight,
and the lost dogs came down from the hills, still lost,
trotting, panting, a tremolo of swollen tongues, their mud-caked
undercarriages swarmed by squadrons of gnats
as dilapidated barns began disappearing at last, swallowed like secrets
by the muck, and the ghosts of handsome assassins
sat up in piles of hay and combed their pompadours
and muttered in Latin their last prayers
before stepping through trapdoors flung open
like flaps of skullskin to the skyblue sky of oblivion—

that same color of your panties, I thought, as you floated topless
across our bedroom in a wake of sparks, a vision sashaying
across the bottom of the sea, visions colliding, the sea rising, please forgive me
my terrors, love, for I saw your braided hair and imagined
a frayed rope lowered from a helicopter, or, worse,
the ropey penis of the horse a general sits in the shade
as bluebottle flies, querulous and fierce, baffle the air
above silhouettes bent digging in a field of clay.
For I watched the sunset so many evenings, holding your hand,
and thought of the combustible blood of an empire,
or lay awake in the long dark listening to your breathing
and imagined sad Abe Lincoln pacing our hallway, his arms folded
behind his back like a broken umbrella, the clock ticking,
the ravenblack sedans idling curbside in the suburbs
of America, watching closely, purring greedily,
as they gulped down the last starlight, dreaming of some other dawn.

Poe Climbs Down from the Long Tapestry of Death to Command an Army of Street Urchins Huddled in the Dusk

You unswaddled, you broken
                bluster of hormones, you smarl
     of flesh sliding down over hip-

bones, woozy with laughter,
               your cheeks splotched purple,
     slubbed with pussy pimples—

You backpack rats, bicycle
               chained, vamped out
     in black drag and combat boots,

jeans ballooning like the bladder of a whale—
               You swaggering insomniacs
     huffing gasoline, flashing your new tats,

cigarettes like lily-stamens
               cupped against the breeze,
     I am climbing down to you

through the phosphorescent dust
               of disappearing ghettos, climbing down
     through torture chambers

in countries somewhere off the map,
               where crocodiles sleep
     curled head-to-tail in claw-footed bathtubs,

exhausted, sated, their titanic snoring
               rattling the pulleys and hooks, rattling
     the long open drawers of knives

and gnarled tools, where starved guinea hens
          lay their periwinkle eggs
       speckled with the blood of those who refused speech—

Climbing down to you, you meth-mouths,
          my darlings of death, your brains
       leaking out through your teeth

as you busk on the boardwalk, butchering
          some Hendrix tune on a two-string ukulele,
       then vanishing beneath the pier

to fuck or piss or cry, as the tide creeps up
          like a thief in the barnacled-dark—
       Down, down, down I come,

my bald head aureoled, following the hair
          of the dead that never stops growing,
       eating the sides of graves,

eating coal, diamonds, scorched tanks; eating voices
          and laughter, tufts of fur, the singing
       of machines, charred referendums, wedding rings,

television antennas like skeletons of early flight;
          eating sheet music, machetes,
       military tents, butchers' aprons, Doric columns,

wristwatches, cancer studies; eating medieval scarecrows;
          eating hospital bills; eating fossils
       of the tiniest oceanic lichen

extinct for millions of years; eating the bloodless
          eyelids of priests and the solid gold
       testicle trusses of generals; eating all of this,

but not the silky, perfumed underthings
of beauty queens and whores
who in death become sleeping angels of memory—

They will remember you, they will remember
this summer, when the heat petrified
the trees, when the river turned

to a long, crazed chessboard of dust
and wharf rats climbed up
through toilets at night, panting, dripping,

sleeping on their backs in the marbled silence
of libraries and museums, while outside
church bells pealed and the war was on

the TV in the window of a rent-to-own store.
A parade crawled past
for those who'd come home blind

or missing an arm or leg or both, shrinking
in their uniforms,
and one of you wept, and another said

the body is a buffet, and someone else said
the mind is a fire escape we piss off of into the darkness
before the cops came to scrub you out,

each of you a speck of yellow vomit caked on the president's lips
the cameras could not witness, you
huddled in the grassy park, high on Vicodin

or Robitussin, *huddled in some séance against freedom*, they said,
the smell of the occult like rancid egg
hanging in the air as you crumpled

beneath the whistling blackjacks, then the *whuck*
               of the body and how they would joke later,
          by God, you doughy freaks, your flesh

like meringue over bone—
               And I heard your cries,
          though I was still so far away, descending

through the intricate, burnt-out circuitry
               of my own brain,
          a head of gelatinous cabbage suspended

in the stupor of memory, dreaming
               of a circus bear I saw once
          sentenced to death in a park in Richmond,

how its handlers, Hungarian twins, paced off ten steps,
               their push broom moustaches twitching
          as they commanded it in their tongue

to stand tall on two legs like a man, and so it did,
               blindfolded, bellowing as it was shot twice
          with a revolver, once by each brother,

first in the heart and at last in the head,
               and even as it staggered it seemed to be
          dancing the rough waltz it knew, and then,

as it fell, it muttered something almost in a woman's voice—
               mea culpa or *sic semper tyrannis*—
          no one could say for sure,

but those who heard it broke out in an icy sweat
               in August and felt a sensation in their bowels,
          something barbed and cold

like the gills of a monstrous catfish—
                  I felt it, yes, the sensation of the heart
            flensed from the head, and the shadows

of both passed through me in one great peristaltic wind
                  that cast my breath down
            like a rotten net into the muck of the body

so that I had to lie down on a bench gasping
                  in the dying light of summer
            as the plucked hearts of the world leapt up

from the grass at dusk, crying out like carbuncular toads,
                  and the severed heads of history
            nodded gently from the branches of the oaks

like so many frostbitten oranges—
                  Yes, I could hear your cries already,
            each of you stretching out

in the narrow corridors of your own pain—
                  you who secretly enjoy algebra;
            you who were a pelican in another life;

you who were a housewife, always sweeping;
                  you who fell in love with a tree
            and told no one;

you who will be killed in war; you who dreamed
                  for weeks on end of turning into a cloud;
            you who will become a priest, a lawyer,

a ballroom dance instructor; you who love the word *dissipation*;
                  you who played a robot in a school play once
            and were happy; you who slit your wrists

and were overcome by the smell of salt,
                    remembering the first time your mother
            held you up in the surf—

Yes, each of you, *e pluribus unum*—glistening
                    from the wounds of Che, Lincoln, Christ,
            where the flesh peeled back smolders

the blue of a Chinese plum and reveals
                    the oblong pearls of putrefaction—
            each of you born again into the grief of a new century,

your cries like feedback trapped inside a syringe,
                    buzzing through my disembodied voice,
            through a dream, through a blip in time,

swirling into a snarling halo of flies that rise from the Bear-
                    of-the-Gone-Gall-Bladder,
            from the spinning plates of the poor,

out of the crushed throats of the disappeared,
                    out of your own mouths that betrayed you—
            Look: some other world, uninhabited

and without speech, turns quietly in your dreams, beveled
                    into vast dimensions of air and light
            and dust. I will lead you there, my darlings.

I am holding you up in my mind:
                    you swarming abattoirs of night,
            you droning calliopes of the dead.

Lullaby for the Last Night on Earth

When at last we whisper, *so long, so lonesome*

and watch our house on the horizon
go down like a gasping zeppelin of bricks,

we'll turn, holding hands,
and walk the train tracks to the sea . . .

So sing me that song where a mountain falls
in love with an octopus, and one thousand fireflies
ricochet around their heads,

and I'll dream we're dancing in the kitchen one last time,
swaying, the window a waystation
of flaming leaves, the dogs shimmying
about our legs,
                        dragging their golden capes of rain . . .

O my critter, my thistle, gal-o-my-dreams,

lift your voice like an oar into the darkness,
for all the sad birds are falling down—

Nothing in this night is ours.

The Last Songbird

We heard you once, here on earth,
    singing from the icy turrets at dawn
  as the tarry wind whipped skyward and you swooped

from steeple to balcony to wire, over the hospital
    where a pink glow pulsed in one window
  like the gummy heart of a mole

that burrows from the center of darkness,
    from the center of stone and clay
  where your song went to perish, how in the end

it already sounded so distant, like the whispers
    of a dying poet trapped inside a glass jar,
  or the sharp gasp of a ghost

bleeding through the radio in an apartment
    where the ceiling kept coughing up
  a fine, stinging snow of asbestos

and we opened the door and heard an explosion
    and we opened the door and the day
  was rubbing its forehead raw in the scalded parking lot

while someone's mother wept, looking for her lost keys,
    O bird, what secrets we could confess
  if only you would hold still, but you keep punishing us

by darting into the gaping mouth of oblivion,
    you keep punishing us, shy thing,
  by turning into a brittle leaf, or by leaping from the edge

of our sight into the cauldron of smoke roiling
    beneath the bridge, punishing us in our dreams
  where you drift and pirouette in the makeshift air,

where you fly in reverse and sing so sweetly
                   that the batik of blood creeping
            over the sidewalk effervesces and recedes, flowing

backwards, and we wake remembering
                   our dead and the bright cafés
            and how we used to whistle a little crooked tune

over the sounds of the morning traffic, calling you
                   down to lift us off the ground a bit
            and bludgeon us with your song.

*

Gorbachev's Ubi Sunt from the Future That Soon Will Pass

I do not know anyone against whom so many slings and arrows have been launched as against Gorbachev at present.

—Mikhail Gorbachev, Memoirs

Where are the snows of yesteryear, Mr. President?

Where are the black sedans, the secret police

dozing behind their sunglasses?

Where are the red telephones gleaming

in half-lit offices, the endless referendums

and memorandums, the long lines for bread and work?

Where are the concrete bunkers, the missiles

ticking beneath their hoods, standing upright and sullen like proud widows?

Where are the white plains of Siberia, the drowsy

plenums in cheap suits, the drones dipping in and out of the clouds?

Where are the jabs, the all-night innuendos over trays of stale Danish?

Ah, yes, Mr. President. In death I speak perfect English.

Ah yes. At heart I was always a poet.

What do I remember?

It was late May, late morning, rain gushing

from the waterspouts, the gutters gurgling like a brook in the Urals.

I was reading my *Memoirs*

for the fourth time, when I felt with much suddenness

the mole of death paddle into the loam of my chest

and then a sensation as if I'd been stretched,

buckled down on a steel table and shot up with osmium,

such heaviness, and then a caving in into blackness and air . . .

Yes, Mr. President. *Glasnost*, too much *glasnost*,

for the One-In-Whom-I-Do-Not-Believe made a gesture

like he was shooting craps in an alley,

and I drifted out of his hand, slowly, into nothingness, into the cold

cataract of space, and I could see him,

the One-In-Whom-I-Do-Not-Believe, I could look

right into his face—flaccid, pale, almost featureless,

as if he'd been scalded by a pot of boiling milk as a child—

and his eyes so sad and bottomless and besotted,

watching Gorbachev watching him in confusion,

and then I could see the One-In-Whom-I-Do-Not-Believe

shake his bald, congealed head, ever so slightly, as if

he pitied Gorbachev, as if he wouldn't gift

a bushel of peasant dung for the hearts of Lenin or Mao,

and I knew then that the One-In-Whom-I-Do-Not-Believe

was a Capitalist, and I turned to you

to say that you could have your Star Wars if the U.S.A.

would show Soviet movies in your picture houses,

for this seemed fair, as we showed many U.S.A. movies

in Soviet picture houses, so I turned to you

but you were not you, Mr. President, you were

a wax replica of you in a cowboy suit

propped in the chair like a corpse, for you could not bend,

and so I then turned to Secretary of State Shultz,

but he was not he, but a thirteen-year-old boy

wearing nothing but a T-shirt and sports socks

masturbating into the lingerie section of a department store catalog,

and I felt ashamed, for the pink of his thighs

reminded me of my auntie's bosom when she bent over to milk the cow,

and outside the snows of Reykjavik

were blotting out the sun, sheeting the windows,

smelting the doors in grey rivulets of ice, and I looked down in terror

at the polished boardroom table and saw myself

in a black mirror surrounded by blackness, surrounded by space,

and I wore a spacesuit lined in lead

to comfort me from the radiation that was no danger,

and it was too hot and I could see the port-wine stain on my forehead

pulsing like an alarm lamp, the archipelago of my fate,

the hotzone of death boring into me.

I had begun to sweat profusely, bilge rising in my boots,

and the various aromas of the afterlife washing over me

like foamy waves. I smelled eggs and potatoes.

I smelled my babushka's ten pewter samovars

soaking in a tub of vinegar. I smelled a cloud of camphor

and tobacco when she lifted her petticoat

to make water, and her black hair

burning like an envelope of forgotten names.

I smelled the mysterious feast in the forest—corned beef,

cabbage, pickled herring, a crystal fingerbowl of honey—

laid out for the flies that worked ceaselessly,

carrying the dead to the living.

I smelled the tears of the starving Poles

weeping by the tracks, and their hands hiding

the wet paper hives of their mouths.

I smelled the dead wasps and the dead leaves.

I smelled the graves opening beneath a blue sky.

They smelled like nothing, like dirt

and crushed chalk and the gluey eyes of the unborn.

I smelled lemon vodka and a vat of soft apples.

I smelled the crozzled skin of the firefighters of Chernobyl.

They were ashamed. Their bodies were still smoking.

I smelled a rose dipped in the blood of the suicides,

and the chemical snows of Kiev,

where children sang, swimming in the river at dusk.

And I smelled the night coming down.

It smelled like gunpowder, like ferocious tumors

fattening in the gelid petri dish of the brain,

as the water crept up, up, up

and I drowned inside my suit, bobbing in my lopsided orbit

while the jaundiced stars burnt out

all around me in one long, broken necklace of exhaust,

and spy satellites tottered overhead

like defunct science projects, their frayed tinfoil,

their twisted coat hangers carrying your voice, Mr. President,

to Gorbachev, your voice so far away, old friend,

how it sounded like it rose from the bottom

of a blighted sea into my helmet, crackling, spiraling

around the thinnest filament of wire, your voice

offering prayers, pledging your help, and I cried out to you then,

for the dead I had denied in life were descending

in a bright crowd, moving through space toward Gorbachev

like a school of luminous jellyfish—

I passed those whose heads

had been airbrushed into oblivion,

how they waved their arms wildly in the emptiness.

I passed the lost cosmonauts of Kapustin Yar,

sibilant and thin, whispering, *Remember us to the Motherland.*

I passed those blindfolded, cigarettes dangling

from their lips, and those who fell in the fields

and rose with poppies in their hair.

I passed the grandmothers of Pripjat, pallid,

doddering, clutching brittle clumps of iron-gray hair

in their fists, and mothers without breasts

who undressed in the dark.

I passed the dropsical lying on gurneys, bellowing

like crippled walruses, peering over the swollen ridges of their flesh.

I passed those who had forgotten how to speak

and those who walked on the knurled stumps of their arms

and those hugging themselves, their skin

sloughing off in saucers of rust.

I passed the strange amalgams, those with dosimeters

for eyes, and those without skulls

whose brains bulged like bulbous potatoes

and asthmatics with long tails, gasping behind their respirators,

and others I could not see, those curdled

into single split seeds of pain, hissing curses only Gorbachev heard . . .

Ah, Mr. President, too much *glasnost*, too much undone.

Where are my tears?

Where is the One-In-Whom-I-Do-Not-Believe?

In my dream of the end he comes to me at last, out of his sickness,

out of his pot of boiling milk, he comes to me

and I say *yes, you are you.* I say, *yes,*

they are mine, I gather them in, and he touches me

and breaks me open like an endless matryoshka full of rain,

and I fall over the scorched forests of Belarus,

where the trees rise like smoke and beings older than man

prick their ears against the silence,

listening for the cries of the idiots and orphans

who move among them now through the unmapped dark.

Silent Montage with Late Reagan in Black and White

He feels the white room
                stuccoed behind his smile—

He feels the silence like an undertow

            of tentacles, and the nurses' hats are canvas sails

scorched with sunlight, gauzy curtains
blousing inside his chest,
                  and when the light at dusk filters

through, it feels like his head is lit by a pot of boiling milk—

He feels the boy take the lens of a projector
into his mouth,

           the cold metal, the heat of the lamp

                       and the white room sinks
into the black Pacific, a rocket, a diving bell,

such emptiness, the earth standing still and the city lights
sizzling out up and down the coast
as water towers topple like B-movie monsters—

Well, he closes his eyes and feels a hollow ringing in his head

           that he keeps falling through, and then a long chorus
of sputtering

like an army of men in a hangar
touching blowtorches to a turbine, and his tongue
palsies, goes gooey and tumescent,
                  a pale sea cucumber asleep in a cave—

What he wanted to say was
that he was handsome once, he was dashing.
That's him jogging across campus at dusk:
white shoes, white pants, three white books
tucked beneath his arm.

He feels matches flare behind his earlobes—

       He feels the shadows of passing cars, finned and purring—

He feels the riptide of minutes, the pot of milk,
         his silence like the lights of a spaceship,

the boy licking his lips and there he goes again
taking the lens into his mouth,
the cold metal, the heat of the lamp . . .

The light passes through them
like a bouncing disco ball, like powdered wigs

     on fire and the boy's lips are big and pouty,

though he's all bones, as if he were slowly sucking up
his flesh through a straw.

      Now the room is lit by a chest X-ray:

grainy fathomlight, shadows
             wavering on the wall
      like scimitars of kelp,
gargantuan forests of sargassum multiplying inside the boy

and the silence won't stop burning
like a city on a hill. It hurts his head to look at him:

    wizened, cheeks phosphorescent, the light
    straining through wobbling cells,

as the men shuffle from the hangar carrying the ringing he keeps
falling through, their paper robes crisp as spacesuits—

> (They cradle blowtorches,
> or are those shapes baby chimps?)

Lesions leech them like the galactic eyes of God,
and they yell at him,
they shake their bony arms . . .

Well, he never found the words
for what he wanted to tell them.

> The days diminish.

The nurses pull the curtain, swaddle his body
in a bleached sheet, and the men come
                        to carry him down into dark water.

They look through him now, as if their blood,
full of stars, is calling them elsewhere.

Love Poem for the Last Night on Earth

When they ask me to account for my time on earth,
I will confess: I loved tomato pie

and too much beer, waking up in the blue
beam of the television, my head in your lap,
how I could hear the last birds
gathering beneath your skin You smelled like mint

and the cold blade of the kitchen knife, and our laughter
left teethmarks those long July days,
as the dark beyond our door culled its armies,

a combustion of insects and heat
hitching our house to the blind grasses, the pasture
sliding away like a calm sea.

Love, what leaned in and drank from the eyes of the horses
as their silhouettes passed like slow ships?
What folded its thin wings and sank into our hearts?

In the City of Fallen Rebels
—after Jaime Sabines

Here comes the boy again, dragging his death

by a string. Here comes the gun he waves above his head.

Here comes the light raked loose

like salted slugs, how it fizzes over liquor bottles

and magazine racks, and he must feel it, yes,

like ulcers puckering his skin, for he hugs himself

with his other arm, high-stepping in place, trying to hold in

the filthy burst mattress of the soul.

But here it comes nonetheless! Christ, look at it!

It won't stop jumping out

to bang on the scuffed Plexiglas window

of heaven. Here come the angels,

they hear him, those starved revenants

trampling the riverbank of his mind. But the gods,

they refuse to blink, *he's nothing more*

than a speck of shit on the eyelash of infinity, they say,

spitting sideways into the dust,

though they come anyway, like Confederate marauders

spurring their wormy, wide-eyed horses

up from the shallow graves.

They're peat burnt and staunch, they're flashing their bleary sabers.

One has a face that keeps fuzzing out,

and one has biceps like a pit bull's flanks splattered with blood,

and when he shoots at them, wailing, bottles explode,

rum tumbles down shelves, trickles

toward the feet of Mrs. Wen.

Here she comes too, fumbling the keys,

trying to coax the register open.

Here come the five English words she knows,

flitting about her like flying mice.

Here come the gods again (they never give up),

and the boiling sargassum of blood she can't hold inside her chest,

as some fusty, ferruginous fog blows in

from the backside of the ghetto.

Here come the dead, they smell it, waking in vacant lots,

shoeless and soft in the weeds. Here come

the screwworms and roaches, the black ocean seething in its bowl

and a whole century like a ship on fire.

In the park, where the boy buys his tinfoil surprise,

the severed heads of history nod all night on their rotten branches.

He blows the gates. He sleeps

his dreamless sleep, curled fetal beneath a bench,

his eyelids blue and blotched with bruises.

Here comes the poet (What does *he* want?).

He's scared of the dark; he'd like to turn into a sparrow,

fly into a steeple, hide beneath a broken bell.

But a desiccated bat hangs at the back of his mind.

He keeps poking it with his pen until the godawful

gods come again (They never quit!).

Here they come, galloping across the river

of a dead king rising, surpliced, bearded in flames,

blowing their battered bugles.

They want a word with the boy, they say. They take him

into the trees. And there he goes, still half-asleep,

dragging his death by a string.

*

Lost on the Lost Shores of New Orleans, They Dreamed Abraham Lincoln Was the Magician of the Great Divide

In unison, the administration unknotted their ties
and rolled up their sleeves
                         and dismissed them into darkness
that was no longer darkness
but a state redefined as *a temporary failure of light*,

though the rain shone on everything like staples that hold
a body together after the soul has slipped out.

They didn't want to be infinite, but more human.
They cried out, placeless and disembodied, scrawling their names
and messages everywhere, a graffiti of prayers pushing
                         back against nothingness, against the rain,

indivisible. The rain behind their eyelids.
The rain pearls of cotton dissolving
                on their chaffed tongues.

They were woe-smitten, a scattered multitude
suddenly visible as if a false wall had fallen, or a green screen
had been flailed diaphanous by the storm, a one-way

window everyone could watch them through,
even as their mouths filled with some stringy albumen of shame and rage,
sour,
        worming up the gullet, forced forward
by the palpitation of disbelief, this latest indignity,

while the sun emerged and bore down on them
like a thumbscrew, like a punctured pouch of embalming fluid,

and the dogs, frantic inside their heads, how they wanted
out, that incessant barking, the raw
paw-pads hanging on, spraddle-legged,
               splayed on the scorched shingles, until finally they knew no one

was coming, and waded into the Great Divide, into that viscous swill
that sawed them in half.

But this was no magic trick,

for there, where the dead bumped, gibbous-eyed, blind as stones,
there where nothing spoke or sang, they could feel

their legs dragged down, scoured logs, bloated pincushions of gout,
a raddled reef of flesh clotting in the murky depths.

They were already ghost-eyed, wandering, their torsos

wimpling, skimming

the septic waterways of their disaster.

Where, we asked, *did they all come from?*

Out of the rain. Out of the ruin.
Out of the hole in his head, their passage paid for
though the past was a sieve

they kept passing through . . .

＊

He pulled his hand out of his hat and the rains

came again. The rain a threshold. The rain snub-nosed.

The rain a shirt coming apart, sodden and sudden.

He was black and seared blacker around the edges.

Jagged. Like a brute

silhouette, a crude paper cutout, or a note

crumpled up, stuffed inside their mouths—

He pulled his hand from his hat and held out the bridge

they'd never make it across, bright lights

and the river braiding its spell of filth beneath it.

He held out questions, unanswerable, and the smell of wet newsprint

that won't wash off. He held out a red scarf,

rigor mortis, a small band of farmers shaking pitchforks at a tank.

He held out two white milk teeth and a bloody teat.

He pulled his hand from his hat and the sky felt like the cool page of a book

when you put your cheek down on it,

and Los Angeles, their love, burned

like a burning bush,

and O! Washington, Detroit, Memphis,

the sun setting, the night sinking behind barricades,

into dumpsters overflowing, into skullcaps sticky, a damask of teargas and sweat.

He held out a gold medal, a fist, mule flies, a white picket fence.

He held out a banjo full of bilge and Big Bill Broonzy

dozing in the back of a gold Cadillac

parked beneath a loblolly, the most beautiful of pines,

spreading, swaying, shading the graves

of the martyrs, and the dust of Jerusalem

they shook from their shoes and the patsy's bullet

plucked out like a dead bumblebee.

He pulled his hand from his hat and they heard the sound of the levee coming apart

like a wave of slurpy thunder, and the pictures of the missing

flapped in the wind and each brick sang out

and they could see in his eyes the black ocean rising

and the light suctioning down

through the grease traps of the inner-ear,

what all snagged there, the unutterable, the grunts, the cries

of surprise the body makes when pierced by fear.

Levitate them, we said,

so he pulled his hand from his hat and held up the hole in his head

they passed through darkly. He held up the paltry

poultice of spit and glue, black armbands

and the splintered leg of the assassin who still wandered there, chagrined, limping.

He pulled his hand from his hat and held up

a canteen of cold water, a bullhorn, and birdsong,

ubiquitous, plumose and transient,

like sea-soaked umbrella seeds dispelled by the wind.

The rain desquamations, the rain strings too short to tie,

twinge of twilight, bluebirds flying backwards

into their nests, disheveled, dragging their ragged ribbons of remembrance,

and the picnic blankets spread out again where they left them

beneath the trees lit up like a shipwreck,

unwavering gangplanks of light, that waxy luminescence,

leaves aglow like candled eggs

and the smell of burning on a Sunday afternoon

when the smoke drifted to them across the tracks,

how they couldn't get it bleached out of their collars.

Look away, look away, he whispered, too breathless to shout, but their eyes hardened already like divots of soured aspic

and we could see in this mass exodus

the vortices they set off in the water and what swam to the surface

in their wake, stubborn and dumb as time itself,

for their old lives, transfigured or ruined, would not perish.

The rain sepia toned. The rain judicious, Bibles bearded in mold, worm-eaten

roses and chipped teacups spinning, auroral,

that taste of resurrection at the back of the throat like chocolate or motor oil.

The rain brusque and somnolent, the deep

ether of wisteria, the spumy billow of bicycle wheels,

and that afternoon, scrubbed-bloodstain-on-the-balcony

rain, curse of their hearts, how he held up

their voices, itinerant, laden with longing, a chorus lifted

high above the shadow of heaven, threading the star that guided them,

crying out again from the scalloped, far edge

of the swamp, the hem of a fever that would not break.

Field Recording, Notes from the Machine

Flip the switch—
    [for fire   for ice]

Flip the switch—
    [and I am a stone in limbo]

Flip the switch—
    [and I am all flawed form   blackedout bluelines   a blurry diagram of chalk]

Flip the switch—
    [and I am a flayed daydream   something barbed and luminous]

Flip the switch—
    [and I am immaculate   tessellated   a sheet-metal overcoat lined in long needles]

Flip the switch—
    [for fever   for tractorlight   for the cold compress of dusk   watch as I dig the pit to slaughter the horses]

Flip the switch—
    [for small miracles   for electricity   for the body open and shut]

Flip the switch—
    [and the buildings sprout]

Flip the switch—
    [for applause   for a tickertape parade   the cerulean sky infinite and without regret]

Flip the switch—
    [and I am invisible]

Flip the switch—
  [and the buildings crumble]

Flip the switch—
  [and they will kneel in the brightshards of glass   they will pick their teeth
  out of the ash]

Flip the switch—
  [for another rendition]

Flip the switch—
  [and some cover their mouths   and some cover their genitals   and some
  cover their breasts]

Flip the switch—
  [and some are in boxes   and some are in piles]

Flip the switch—
  [and my mind is a missile   a green light threading a sleeping chimney]

Flip the switch—
  [and my mind is a bucket and a board]

Flip the switch—
  [and I'll put their eyes out with a spoon and a song]

Flip the switch—
  [and I'll pour my cold blood into the astonished asshole of the mouth]

Flip the switch—
  [and they will mistake me for the sea   for something alive   for something
  that cares]

Visions for the Last Night on Earth

That spring the wind smelled like a bag of loose nails, and the sky kept turning a candied, gaseous green like a film of algae blooming in a plastic wading pool. Each morning we awoke to some new sign. Once, for instance, piles of dogshit furred in a dewy-white mold rose from the yard like the ruins of a forgotten civilization that orange butterflies visited, rowing their wings triumphantly in the watery sunlight. Another morning we spied on our neighbor shirtless in his driveway, stroking his scumbled beard, standing amidst his fleet of rusted-out jalopies, one arm extended as though to shake hands with a delegation of ghosts. That spring the beehives collapsed, along with several celebrities, a handful of foreign governments, an ancient glacier, a foolproof military strategy, a small enclave of albino badgers, a respected Mexican drug cartel, a friend's vegetable garden, and a senator from some-such-place. Some degenerate began stalking you, too, and when you pointed him out and I stalked him back across campus, I couldn't stop myself from thinking that he looked like a terrorist. Sorrow and fear sawed us in half, love, like a broken zipper, and sometimes, in the middle of the afternoon, we locked the bedroom door and held each other with the lights on, the room so cramped and stuffy it was like being marooned in a space capsule drifting out of orbit, further away from the world, though the storms blew in again and we could hear the water rising in the basement. Once, curled there with you, afraid to move lest the house slide off its foundation, I heard the dog make a percolating noise in his lungs like oil bubbling up through hot sand, and then he sighed so deeply I imagined his bones filling with air, and then you mumbled in your sleep, *I only want to keep from disappearing.* I felt a vibration behind my eyes like a manhole cover clanging shut, and I slept and dreamed I was crawling headfirst through the basement or a cave or the hold of a wrecked ship, drawn forward by the bouncing fulcrum of my flashlight. Ahead of me I could see the ground writhe with speckled salamanders, blind and mercurial, silver driblets gnawing at the damp edges of my shadow. When I touched one it sprouted eyes in the darkness. I felt it watching me. I felt the future, alien and indifferent, like the sump of its cold, liquid heart racing beneath my fingertip.

Field Recording, Billie Holiday from the Far Edge of Heaven

Loverman, when I woke
we were banished

on a rooftop together,
the city sopped up by the sea.

The hours unfolded twice, and you
torqued skyward like Atlas holding up
the moon the whole lonely night.

I begged on those stars.
I sang, *I aint got no change in my pocket,*
Mister Trenchcoat, I aint got no galloping white horse

but they kept hammering in the attics,
they cried out like lions to their Lord . . .

Darling boy, we were drowning
in our own embrace,

and beneath those sodium flares
of sleep I kept dreaming
we were the lucky ones at last,

lifting off like two pelicans
that plummet for the same spangled fish.

Nightmare for the Last Night on Earth

Through the hole in the back of my head
I could see the room—
a metal bed, hooks, a pulley, a tub of water.

The light flickered—
                    fissured, vertiginous,
as if a Ferris wheel churned
inside the cement wall.

In the shadows, a hooded man handcuffed to a radiator.
He was sprawled in a dark puddle.
He was so small, he was disappearing, his ribs
glistened like black grains of rice . . .

I heard chattering in the distance,
something guttural and moist, like an army
of worms tunneling through the white screen of sleep,
their soft beaks scraping the windowpane . . .

I opened my mouth and nothing came out—

This was the last acquiescence:
my silences rose to heaven like handkerchiefs on fire.

*

A Brief Oral Account of Torture Pulled Down Out of the Wind

[What the Hood Whispers to the Head]

friend I grow more alive with you each day

I drink up your sweat your spit your tears

I drink up your grey phlegm and the blistered coagulations of blood

minerals once a part of you

fizz between us like cold starlight

scouring the desert and when you drown

in the long keelhaul of electricity

I suck in your breath

that prickly chandelier of wind

shuddering from your throat

believe me when I say that there are things

you do not want to see

your body is eating itself

and still they grin they strike a pose for the camera

when they wring me out they'll know

I held your dreams

like a bell holds the iron ghost of sound

[*What the Dog Whispers to the Shape Cowering in the Corner*]

and now I'm drenched at the end of my chain

truculent implacable circling inside

the shape your fear makes

lunging toward that cloudy omphalos

of scent that plumbs you like a poisoned well

tang of urine tang of sweat

blowback of pheromones rising

in corpuscles of oil ripe with the soured colostrum

of your beginning

this is our first and only dalliance

for we're off and running headlong downhill

through some bottomless perdition

statues topple songbirds plummet from the sky

generals hide beneath their overcoats

clouds boil then blot out the sun

whole continents fall away beneath our feet

and when you turn to face me at last

you will face the gnawed synapses of memory

rising mercurial from the deep

brine-flooded folds of your own brain

gathering into a throbbing body of froth

gathering into a windbent wound sprouting teeth

you will weep

you will call it dog

you will kneel and rise and kneel again

you will devour yourself in your dreams

[What the Boot Whispers to the Heart Beneath Its Heel]

at night through the crack below the door

I've glimpsed you floating in the air above the body

drenched with a vermillion glow

the whole cell gliding beneath your light

I've dreamt of throngs of you

rising unabated through the calm of sleep

hearts of string and papier-mâché

stuffed with the offal of goats or chickens

humming chanting stammering on the vulgar parlance

of the backward and the dead

of devious sodomites that starve themselves for their sins

of djinns sidling through subway tunnels

drawing their bristling tails up beneath their robes

one flinch and the hemispheres are riven

sliding into the hardscrabble abyss of your caesura

one flinch and whole civilizations are buried in sand

believe me when I say that such figments

of the imagination will be squashed with impunity

I will kick you back across the precipice of illusion

I will marry you to the earth

or hold you down squirming until my master

places you in the middle of a cold tray

fool you have neither wings nor feet

and I have no heart

yet see how I gleam without it

[What the Torturer Whispers to Himself in the Mirror]

whence the fuck have we come to this place

to this godawful understory of the unrighteous

where the nightsky looks like some putrid ocean drying up

and the air itself stops up the breath

like wading through static through a thousand broken voices

a scourge of suffocating ghosts languishing in the heat

and despite it all we sleep the sleep of the just

dreaming of the cunts of Istanbul

a whole harem calling out to us wraithlike

across mountains and the vast expanse of empty desert

whispering to us through a veil of hookah smoke and silk scarves

until we rise in darkness at last without rebuke

hardened by what we forego invoking the fear of our people

invoking the columns of fire and ash

even as the low concussions in the east

reverberate bellowing those spineless simians

from their mudhuts and holes those muddleheaded mopes

that they bring here to cower and slobber

and sink into a pile of their own shit

listen we are beholden to no one we are without peer

without recompense we have pledged our troth to the one god

and the one country and to each other

and still there is this monumental boredom this loneliness

this squat cinderblock prison the TV nowhere

a garble of pixels the flies the fetid stink

of the weak and the mad

some nights a sunburnt lieutenant drops by to give orders

or to laugh raucously at his own dirty jokes

some nights we drink and wait for the phone to ring

some nights we burn sodden mattresses

books photos clothes of the dead

or sit gasmasked shooting at animals

scurrying across the lunar landscape of the lost

but listen tonight we'll redeem the names

of our fathers tonight we'll rise up

shirtless lipsticked levitating in front of the mirror

brandishing our cocks in our rubbergloved fists

the dogs whimper pace inside their cages

through the walls we can hear our enemies crying out

[What the Prisoner Whispers into the Ears of the Sleepers]

cold sleepless I drift beneath the hood

and dream the silence is a glass ship

descending from the fathoms of outerspace

then occasionally a burst of laughter

from another room or a blunt yowl

and I remember my face reflected back at me

from the gleaming surface of a boot

like the enormous wizened face of a squid

at the bottom of a black ocean drying up

once I dreamt my body

was a life raft on fire or a bed going up in flames

and my heart flew above me like a wet kite

as I paddled with all my remaining strength

through my village through refugee camps

through foreign cities dissolving on the wind

I kept passing you

you had been to market you looked besieged

by boredom so small

inside your clothes you couldn't lift your eyes

what I wanted to say was this

once in the beginning I dreamt of you

surging over a hill singing your voices

welded together in the air

you were defiant and mysterious

you were a crush of candlelight at the gates

[What the Fly Whispers to the Voices in the Wall]

once when you could not lift your arms

I partook of your bodies

now you're no more than puddles trapped in stone

forgive me my old opprobriums

as even tonight I'm about my father's business

the world churns on

through endless joy and oblivion

so speak to me now as you disappear

and I will carry your message

to the cold lips of the sleepers

yes I will tell them I saw you standing amazed

smiling in another life

I will look them in the eye

I will tell them you longed to be loved

NOTES

The poems in this collection were begun in June 2004 and finished in December 2008.

"Dragging Canoe Vanishes from the Bear Pit into the Endless Clucking of the Gods": Some of this poem's imagery originates from my childhood memories of visiting the bear pits in Cherokee, North Carolina—homemade attractions created as a source of tourist income by members of the Eastern Band of the Cherokee Nation. When "problem" black bears ventured down out of the mountains to raid dumpsters, they were often captured and placed in these pits for viewing. In 1775, at the Treaty of Sycamore Shoals, the Cherokee sold a huge portion of their land (what is now central Kentucky and north central Tennessee) to the Transylvania Land Company. Many believe that the presiding chiefs were coerced or manipulated with rum. At the final feast and signing of the treaty, Dragging Canoe, a Cherokee warrior, rose in angry protest, vowing to turn the land into a "dark and bloody ground." He formed the Chickamauga Confederacy—the first indigenous resistance movement—which consisted of Cherokees, Choctaws, Chickasaws, Creeks, Shawnees, freed Blacks and some three hundred British Tories, and led attacks on white settlements in his old homeland for the next seventeen years. In 1792, after dancing all night to celebrate an alliance with the Mississippi Choctaw, Dragging Canoe collapsed and died at the age of fifty-four. In 1838, under President Andrew Jackson's Indian Removal Act, over seventeen hundred Cherokee were removed from their homes at gunpoint, put into stockades in holding camps with only the clothes on their backs, and then eventually marched on foot some twelve hundred miles away to what is now Oklahoma. An estimated four thousand Cherokee died on what's known as The Trail of Tears. The last two lines of section four echo Derek Walcott's "The Schooner 'Flight'": "I have either Dutch, nigger, and English in me, / and either I'm nobody, or I'm a nation."

"Gorbachev's Ubi Sunt from the Future That Soon Will Pass": The Chernobyl nuclear reactor disaster—the world's worst nuclear accident—occurred on April 26, 1986, badly contaminating large areas of the former Soviet Union (including Russia, Ukraine, and Belarus). Over 330,000 people were displaced, and the United Nations dubbed the explosion "the greatest environmental catastrophe in the history of humanity." The effects of the radioactive fallout continue to sicken and kill those exposed and their children. This poem is indebted to the photography of Paul Fusco and the transcripts of the talks between President Reagan and Secretary General Gorbachev on the Star Wars Defense Initiative that took place in Reykjavik, Iceland, in October 1986. The lines "her black hair / burning like an envelope of forgotten names" are adapted from Frank Stanford's *The Battlefield Where the Moon Says I Love You* (Lost Road Publishers, 2000).

"Silent Montage with Late Reagan in Black and White": Although the first documented cases of AIDS came in 1981, Ronald Reagan remained silent on the epidemic for most of his presidency, not giving a major policy speech that addressed the disease until October 1987. By the end of that year, there were more than seventy-one thousand reported AIDS cases in the United States, and at that point, over forty-one thousand men, women, and children had already died.

"Lost on the Lost Shores of New Orleans, They Dreamed Abraham Lincoln Was the Magician of the Great Divide" is dedicated to the memory of those who died in Hurricane Katrina, which made landfall on August 29, 2005.

"Nightmare for the Last Night on Earth" and "A Brief Oral Account of Torture Pulled Down Out of the Wind" are both indebted to Roberto Bolaño's *By Night in Chile* (New Directions, 2003) and to the paintings of Fernando Botero and Leon Golub.

Other Books in the Crab Orchard Series in Poetry

Muse
Susan Aizenberg

Lizzie Borden in Love:
Poems in Women's Voices
Julianna Baggott

This Country of Mothers
Julianna Baggott

The Sphere of Birds
Ciaran Berry

White Summer
Joelle Biele

Rookery
Traci Brimhall

In Search of the Great Dead
Richard Cecil

Twenty First Century Blues
Richard Cecil

Circle
Victoria Chang

Consolation Miracle
Chad Davidson

The Last Predicta
Chad Davidson

Furious Lullaby
Oliver de la Paz

Names above Houses
Oliver de la Paz

The Star-Spangled Banner
Denise Duhamel

Smith Blue
Camille T. Dungy

Beautiful Trouble
Amy Fleury

Soluble Fish
Mary Jo Firth Gillett

Pelican Tracks
Elton Glaser

Winter Amnesties
Elton Glaser

Strange Land
Todd Hearon

Always Danger
David Hernandez

Red Clay Suite
Honorée Fanonne Jeffers

Fabulae
Joy Katz

Cinema Muto
Jesse Lee Kercheval

Train to Agra
Vandana Khanna

If No Moon
Moira Linehan

For Dust Thou Art
Timothy Liu

Strange Valentine
A. Loudermilk

Dark Alphabet
Jennifer Maier

Oblivio Gate
Sean Nevin

Holding Everything Down
William Notter

American Flamingo
Greg Pape

Crossroads and Unholy Water
Marilene Phipps

Birthmark
Jon Pineda

Threshold
Jennifer Richter

On the Cusp of a Dangerous Year
Lee Ann Roripaugh

Year of the Snake
Lee Ann Roripaugh

Misery Prefigured
J. Allyn Rosser

Roam
Susan B. A. Somers-Willett

Persephone in America
Alison Townsend

Becoming Ebony
Patricia Jabbeh Wesley

A Murmuration of Starlings
Jake Adam York

Persons Unknown
Jake Adam York